MORE PRAISE FOR *NOW THESE TH*

Few times do I read a book of poems and feel
of something larger. In *Now These Three Rema*
poems pull the reader deep into the moment, and *all your old dreams & your
beforelife & your afterlife* exist around you. With intriguing and engaging lines
like *I want to hold onto the person/I was a week ago* and *What is beautiful can
be pulled into an undertow,* Snyder moves us into a world of the sacred, into a
deeper connection with our daily lives. Compassion is a lifeline through this
gorgeous collection with faith telling us: *When you hold onto the strong thread,
you unbury yourself.* These poems are a beautiful meditation with meaning –
perceptive and connective – this is a book you will return to; *Now These Three
Remain* is Snyder at her very best. I am so thankful these poems are in the world
and highly recommend this collection for every bookshelf. These are the poems
you need to read when you want to remember that there is so much more.
— **Kelli Russell Agodon**, *Dialogues with Rising Tides* (Copper Canyon Press)

NOW THESE THREE REMAIN

SARAH DICKENSON SNYDER

For Joe —
So nice to meet you
Go Reading! :)

Sarah

LILY POETRY REVIEW BOOKS

Library of Congress Control Number: 2022948844

Cover design and Layout: Michael d'Entremont McInnis

ISBN: 978-1-957755-09-0

Published by Lily Poetry Review Books
223 Winter Street
Whitman, MA 02382
https://lilypoetryreview.blog/

...faith, hope, and love, but the greatest of these is love. 1 Corinthians 13:1

for Ben, Abby, & David: these three, who teach me about love

CONTENTS

Un/Faith

When God Listens to Eve 3
Landing 5
You Will Find It 6
I am From the Church of Human Hands 7
Departure Language 9
Now A Hospice Volunteer 10
In the Butterfly Pavilion 11
Field Birds After the Rain 12
A Vanishing 13
The Meet Up 14
To Follow Undisciplined Ink or Having Many Things to Carry 15
To See the Healing 16
Night Work 17
Come Close 18
On Leaving 19
Maine Coast 20
Our Holy Symbols Need Attention 21
Where We Might Go 22

Un/Hope

Squall 24
Entering *The Odyssey* 25
Inauguration 2020 26
The History of Humans, I Mean Plants, I Mean Humans 27
The Way He Saved Blue 28
The Landscape Emerging 29
After Two Years of Reading Heather Cox Richardson 30
After Us 31
Traveling 32

On the Bank   34
At Nyamata   35
That's What It Is   36
Hope Rising   37
Stonework   38
Industry   40
Letterpressing in Autumn, 2020   41
We Were Here   42

    Un/Love

An Index of Sorrow   44
Ginger Roots   45
Without Regret   46
What the Astronaut Finds   47
The Strong Thread   48
Before the Currents in My Blood Began   49
Maybe It Started with the Composition Book   50
The Parade   51
Temple   52
Inhabiting an Ant   53
Interpreter   54
God   55
My Anatomy   56
Riddles   57
A Young Man Sits Beside Me on the Stone Bench at
    The Killing Fields   58
Daybreak   59
Giving Thanks   60
Making Sense   61
In Search Of   63

With gratitude to the publications in which the following poems, sometimes in different versions, first appeared:

433 Journal: "Where We Might Go" & "Riddles"
Art on the Trails 2020 & 2021: "Hope Rising" & "To See the Healing"
Atlanta Review: "Without Regret"
Autumn Sky Daily: "Inhabiting an Ant"
Buddhist Poetry Review: "Traveling"
Derailleur Press: "To Follow Undisciplined Ink or Having Many Things to Carry"
Free State Review: "The History of Humans, I Mean Plants, I Mean Humans" & "Squall"
Gleam: Journal of the Cadralor: "In Search Of"
Hare's Paw Literary Review: "Departure Language"
Indolent Books: "Stonework" & "Letterpressing in Autumn, 2020"
Iron Horse Literary Review: "Ginger Roots" & "Come Close"
isacoustic: "On the Bank"
Kosmos: journal for global transformation: "Industry"
Lily Poetry Review: "Daybreak" & "An Index of Sorrow"
Literary North: "Maybe It Started with the Composition Book"
Lunch Ticket: "Inauguration 2021"
Midway Journal: "Giving Thanks"
Mom Egg Review: "The Parade" & "God"
Nelle: "Departure Language"
The New Verse News: "Maine Coast"
One Art Journal: "Night Work" & "Our Holy Symbols Need Attention"
One Sentence Poems: "On Leaving"
Pangyrus: "Landing" (nominated for a Pushcart Prize)
Persimmon Tree Literary Magazine: "Temple"
Press Pause Press: "Making Sense"
Quartet: "The Meet Up"
Radar Poetry: "The Landscape Emerging"
Rattle: "I am From the Church of Hands"
RHINO: "Entering *The Odyssey*"

scissors & spackle: "The Way He Saved Blue"
Rogue Agent: "A Vanishing"
South Florida Poetry Journal: "My Anatomy"
SWWIM: "Field Birds After the Rain" & "Now a Hospice Volunteer"
Terrain: "After Two Years of Reading Heather Cox Richardson"
Typishly: "We Were Here"
Wax Poetry and Art: "That's What It Is"

Awards:

2021 White Award, Poetry Society of Vermont: "In the Butterfly Pavilion"

NOW THESE THREE REMAIN

UN/FAITH

WHEN GOD LISTENS TO EVE

It's hard to be the beginning
the one pulled from a cage of ribs
without the sweet smell of milk
or symbiosis of skin,
that's probably why he and I began
our cleaving, arriving already
long-limbed and flat bellied.
The only sanity would be to sleep
next to him, to reach and find
spaces in our darknesses under the stars.
Both of us motherless.
I wander on the spongy soil
where there's too much to harvest,
every tree humming
with wind and bird sound.
Ferns unfurled and generous.
And those leafy walls of scent:
lilac, jasmine, and their shadows.
All the furred and winged animals
seem indifferent and ornamental.
I count the loud crows without number,
follow their spiriting from branch to sky.
And when I look beyond to the changing moon
barely there in blueness,
I am surrounded and uncertain.
I need to know the world of same
that comes from same.
A seed begets a tree, a tree its fruit.
Every stone stays in a perfect place
except the small, smooth ones I pick up.
        Maker, the next time

you want to make yourself into flesh
and blood again, place us in a mother,
let us collapse into her arms
and know the watermark
of a child's tears from birth.

LANDING

This was before the angels
saved me on the dark corridor
of highway, before the acres
of pain, how I wanted to shout,
Why do we have to die?

I whispered, *Heal us, heal us*
hoped my words found an ear,
imagined rising like mist –
how easy it used to be as a child.
The ritual of bended knees, my head leaning
on tethered palms against my bed, and what
had I said – some small psalm
to the celestial back then?

I remember flying in a thunderstorm –
the other passengers slept or read
while I was desperate to hold
hands with a stranger in the dark
disturbance, barnacle myself
to another to keep us whole.

YOU WILL FIND IT

What is beautiful can be pulled into an undertow
or become part of the falling water from a fountain,

the deep strangeness of stone's skin,
a body frozen

as if all timepieces vanished and there is only one shape
against a purpling sky in the stilled world.

That moment of song when the chorus finds
its oneness or that echoing note that rings

inside a bronze bell. Bruises heal
and scars tighten into thin lines

from a wide wedge of blood and sever.
Be silent. Wait for what you know is there.

I AM FROM THE CHURCH OF HUMAN HANDS

the Hands that tighten the lug bolts on rotated tires,
the Hands that picked the hen-of-the woods
(and not death caps) I buy to make wild mushroom soup,
the hundreds of steady Hands clasping steering wheels on a highway,
the Hands of Lucille Clifton, Emily Dickinson, and Kay Ryan
the Hands of the surgeon who replaced my worn knee bones with titanium
the Hands of the man unearthing and fixing the water pipe to the house
the Hands of the engineer who designed the bridge I drive over every day
and the Hands of the ones who built it
the Hands of the pharmacist who counts out the right pills
the Hands of the assembly worker who attached my brakes
the Hands of lighthouse keepers, beacons in the fog and darkness
the Hands of my sisters who make beautiful things
the Hands that pick up the injured, move them to safety
the Hands of the women who forge paths through the uncharted
the Hand that holds a flaming torch on the edge of a country
the Hands that cooked the red Thai curry I ate last night
the Hands of my father, strong, warm, and kind
the Hands that planted daffodils, peonies, & blue irises I see each spring
the Hands that met me out of the womb
the Hands of the woman who cuts my hair
the Hands of Georgia O'Keefe, Mary Cassatt, and Picasso
the Hands of the rescuers after an avalanche
the Hand of the man in the ambulance who said, *We've got you.*
the Hands of my mother, making clothes, sweaters, and chicken cordon bleu
the Hands of my students, raised and ready to speak
the Hands of my children, so small at first
the Hands of you, how grateful I am –
I have faith in what Hands do.
Picture this scene in the Church
of Human Hands – our cupped Hands

holding holy water and maybe we Hand out
Hand-outs, and Hands-down,
everyone gets a Hand or lends a Hand.
Hand over Hand, we rise, do our jobs,
hold Hands or clap our Hands, pressed
together – our best, close at Hand.

DEPARTURE LANGUAGE

They say great athletes visualize success,
to will themselves into win. I visualize
the worst so that I know how to survive,
see myself in the tumult of an avalanche
feel the stillness of a white world
and then drool to feel where gravity
takes the little rivulet on my frightened skin
and dig in the opposite direction.
I keep a tool in my glove compartment
to smash the car window
in case I plummet into water.
Into the terrible not.

NOW A HOSPICE VOLUNTEER

How shocked I was
as a child to learn
that the architecture
of life included
a crumbling.

How now each dying
is a softer echo –
the way veins
of a fallen leaf
are a faint imprint
of the tree
or the inside whorl
of a shell still holds
onto the sea.

Each time.

IN THE BUTTERFLY PAVILION

One settles on my finger,
its wings twinned fans,
a lightness before it lifts –

what occurs in the chrysalis
may be proof enough –
the dissolving into a slurry of atoms,
the spin & surge & turn –
an imaginal unfolding into flying –

that we might soar beyond
our slow crawl so close
to the earth, move from
one kind to a higher kind,
find that we are winged.

FIELD BIRDS AFTER THE RAIN

Lately I've been watching
them, the way the juncos
seem to know my home,
every stretch of the deck
railing they claim, the way they turn
toward me at the kitchen window.

Look, three sparrows
on the sagging wet wire of patio lights,
how they sway and hold on
to such a narrow perch.

They welcome the weight
of water. They have
their own atmosphere,
their own moon.

A VANISHING

I can't remember when exactly
I stopped believing I had
magical powers,
                    but maybe
it was that day walking home alone
from school and two boys
leaped from the woods,
pinned me down in the dirt
and leaves and pine needles –
it must have been fall.
Their mouths taking
all of the oxygen,
their laughter and running
away, my re-entry shadowed
with a sky inscribed by branches,
sitting up and brushing off,
my mouth still feeling
like something was there.

I remember the seconds
of not-breathing, those seconds
falling inside me like a rock in a pond,
settled in the muck but still there
to see whenever the water clears.

And never telling anyone.
Making it just a kiss
as if a kiss would feel like that.

THE MEET UP

I have started laying out my clothes for the day
on the just-made bed: jeans, t-shirt, sweater,
underwear, and the warm socks, two commas
on top of the comforter. I'm amused,
this channeling of my middle school self:
that perfect gray V-neck sweater, the plaid skirt,
and white knee socks.
But a meeting with you, God,
I'm not sure what I'd wear, not sure I would forgive you –
I'm thinking of genocides, how many there've been;
and these past four years and this last endless one –
too many taken, how much of me
was built on joy and has collapsed. I doubt
I'll show up – it was in a cathedral, right?
Why such a big house and so much light?

TO FOLLOW UNDISCIPLINED INK OR
HAVING MANY THINGS TO CARRY

Think of all the things to save:
those sheets of shirt cardboard,
the *Rabbit, rabbit*s I say aloud
to no one on the first day
of every month, the embroidered fabric
I found in the night market of Chiang Mai,
pens with thin nibs, what my mind finds
like a planet devoted to spinning,
that miniature metal sculpture of a woman
riding a bicycle the back flap of her dress
curled from imagined wind in Vietnam,
pockets of letters, the tile from Istanbul
symmetrical and filled with hues of blues
like my daughter's eyes & her voice in the dark
at four-years-old, *I don't want to die
alone*, and the fact that each kernel
of corn is attached to a thread of silk
under the husk. Maybe the end
will be like diving into a channel
with a shore on the other side
that we don't know is reachable.
Maybe we'll carry what we've saved
as we fall into water or become water
falling or at least feel touched
by its weight, its glistening,
that last breath unribbed.

TO SEE THE HEALING

Now that the wildflowers have come up
and ferns unfurled in the soft ruffle of new grass,
it doesn't look like destruction, but trees were wounded,
their stumps and roots a testament to what once stood.
I can almost see the stitched leaves and branches
when I look up into the open sky.
The earth heals itself and so do we.
The burned blister on my knuckle still glistens
with something like blood, but new skin is weaving
itself together. This small healing makes me believe
in a god more than all the hours I spent
on a wooden pew where I played hangman
with my sister on the back of the Sunday program.
And now to wake up, fine, the way the earth pulls off
its lid of ice and lilacs burst their heavy purple lungs,
the way a desert can yield a succulent or an armadillo.
We can mend. Even the worst
diagnosis can be rinsed of almost-death.
The fear of leaving leaves, hope returns.
It's my favorite epic simile in *The Odyssey*
when Penelope first speaks to the old beggar
who is Odysseus transformed by Athena
to mete out justice – *as the snow melts,*
mountain streams run full: so her white cheeks
wetted by these tears. Somehow she knows
she is with him.

NIGHT WORK

In the lucid hours of insomnia
I build and multiply images –
a whole wall of unsleeping,

feel the stillness
of my husband's body
against my unspooling.

I lift the necklace of marigolds,
a gift in Rishikesh, almost inhale
the-more-dirt-than-flower scent.

Now I'm on our road at dusk
in that echo of one gunshot.
It's hunting season, everyone

wearing red or orange.
Where did that bullet land,
did it sink in living skin?

I am on a mission
to dig and dig
until the clink of bone,

and I find the rhyme
in *love* and *blood*.

COME CLOSE

I want to hold onto the person
I was a week ago, the one
who remembered not to eat,
who washed her body clean
with antiseptic soap,
who stood in watery silence
as the suds sank in before rinsing,
who patted her body dry,
who would soon walk down the stairs
out into the wide morning air
not really brave but finding
something like faith.
For this moment though
she sat naked on the just-made bed,
bent her left knee close to her face
and kissed the taut skin
over the old bones
that would soon be replaced
and whispered, *Thank you*
like a prayer.

ON LEAVING

I will miss
even cleaning
the lint screen
each time I do
laundry, feeling
the mesh on my fingertips –
doing something I know
will lengthen the life
of a machine.

MAINE COAST

Pleated in every human minute
is the second of someone's death –
the way a mother and daughter leap
from a warm wooden dock
into the Maine coast sea
and the mother is taken
in the sharpness of a second –
the shark's desire to clench
what looked like seal skin. What if
she had not worn the wet suit, what if
they had decided to eat lunch before
the swim – sandwiches
& iced tea on the deck, what if
clouds obscured the sun & they hadn't
needed relief from heat, what if
we knew the second of our leaving,
could stop ourselves
from diving in.

OUR HOLY SYMBOLS NEED ATTENTION

As a child I was horrified when I walked into church
and saw a poor man hanging from a cross, those drips

of blood caught in time at the center of his palms,
nails through them and his crossed ankles, his head bent

in death. A murder scene at the end of a red-carpeted aisle.
Then onto the bread I watched people eat that I could not have.

A piece of his body. And the tray of money, something else
I could not have as it passed by. Too much to store in a brain

stacking itself with fears. Those pipes blaring a hymn,
my mother's voice otherworldly as she stood next to me.

WHERE WE MIGHT GO

Rise to a passing cloud,
slurry into unencumbered
atoms, settle into deepness
of dirt or sea, see a god,
sit among rocks, breathe
as a body could not,
barnacle onto wing,
float in acres and acres
of air, release need,
know before-rain,
& bloom what shined inside.

UN/HOPE

SQUALL

On the cusp of summer
the snow looks weary, reluctant.

We have gone
over a cliff's edge

like the dream I had last night,
my car veering off the road,

almost too frightening
to write down.

My mind swerves away
as I wish the car had,

wish the world had,
wish we had a Greek Chorus

to guide us in unison.
A voice. A compass. Aeneas.

I want the simple texture
of living, something to touch –

that red velvet my mother
stitched into a dress.

ENTERING *THE ODYSSEY*

I like thinking of Penelope,
watching her weave and unweave,
maybe see Athena slip into her
room, hover over the bed built
into a tree, ease her into dream.
See the stone ledge of her window
lined with a white-tipped feather,
milky curves of shells, and small bones
like something on our kitchen sill –
a wishbone among the dust
and keys and curled rubber bands.
The furcula, what a bird needs to pull its wings
up and down. My mother dried it
in the sun, the arched "v" reminding me
of the skeletal remains of a tiny angel's
cast-off wings, where it awaited
the breaking and wish-granting.
The weight of waiting, of anticipating
who gets the larger part, my small
index finger being brave,
willing to have a wish unmet.
So much in what vanishes, too much to count –
who has more cherry pits in the bottom of her bowl,
who gets the paper ring of a grandfather's cigar,
who holds her breath the longest in that under-
world of water – will we ever get what we want?
Maybe all hope is an old beggar.

INAUGURATION 2020

The afternoon's last light feels like a divine hand,
not like the ropey veined one I see taking my mind
across a page, no, it is smooth and glowing exactly
as I imagined some god's hand with a sound
of leaving, gentle and kind, the way I hope
mine is to my kids over the phone, the way I say,
I would love you even if you weren't my child, my love
like a gesture from a star hand.

How do stars look
in outer space, do they get lost in the darkness
and the light of one large star, that fist of fire
I need like water. Do you know that tears
need gravity to fall? In space they congeal
into drops and sink back into eyes, stinging
on re-entry. I wonder about the astronaut
who shared this fact – her shade of grief.

And why haven't I cried until today
when I sang along with Garth Brooks,
my husband, too, him singing and crying,
a man who won't dance with me in our kitchen
in case someone sees him through the window.
We both sang, *I once was lost, but now I am found*, crying
because grief and relief finally rhymed with grace.

THE HISTORY OF HUMANS, I MEAN PLANTS, I MEAN HUMANS

As in how lichens
thrive on bare rock –
how little is needed
to breathe. Even if
trespassed or scraped,
skin heals, knuckles
bend again. We're all
susceptible to injury,
knees lose their fluidity,
eyes die from within,
but mending and living
pull us up from the mud
toward a sun we do not see –
a warmth, one person's kindness,
one person in a sea
of others walking by
or turning away, just one
who stops, leans into us,
offers a hand, a word,
or maybe just the invisible
tie of eyes.

THE WAY HE SAVED BLUE

after Spencer Finch's "Trying to Remember the Color
of the Sky on That September Morning"

Say the unerased.
Say the unimaginable stilled.
Say that blue as a new color, as if it could stay.
Say rows and rows of thousands of shades
of blue are placeholders for what has no words.
Say the remembered.
Say the slate I carve is a stone tablet.
Say the way I press ink into paper.
Say the only thing I know is touch.
Say I am animal with tools.
Say the terracotta pots are gardens.
Say apple. Say pomegranate.
Say blue over & over & it will.
Say blossom and leaf to the wolf
of dust & smoke & remains.

THE LANDSCAPE EMERGING

The leaves are leaving
as if the soil needs to eat yellow and red
and orange, as if the ground didn't have enough
fire, as if there weren't already a molten belly
in all of us hungry for god hearts and the sheen
of words. Is every hour a feeding hour?
I remember hunger swelling into sunflower.
Upturned and eating husk and seed.
Please was the wellspring of swallow.
I was the between with something living,
refilling, waiting in a room of me.
Was she homesick for the stars?
A billion cells boundless,
exactly perfect and tiny
like a bird. Let's say I gave way,
my body elastic. She into she
we into her, her spilled
into the glossary of born.

AFTER TWO YEARS OF READING
HEATHER COX RICHARDSON

I cannot tell if we are on the verge
of another ending, the way we lost
a collective innocence in the blue
blue sky on 9/11. Today humans stir their fear
and wrath with guns and rights, icebergs melt
and hurricanes and tornadoes whip the fiery wind,
floods and virus fill our streets, and truth
seems obsolete – is this the beginning
of another end? I remember my mother saying,
Well, if worse comes to worst, we can always...
She had a plan, had something
to defrost in the freezer, knew how
to avoid cops as she sped along the highway.
Now she's hushed in the sediment
of our pond – her ashes billowed into a ghost
before they settled. Is the world unspooling
its heft as it spins and tilts into disaster?
I want it to last. I want pesto and breath
and maybe a few grandchildren
who will swim, held in the cool water,
a clear sky rippled on the surface.

AFTER US

The earth is all that lives.
It & the stars

speak in an alphabet of green
and dotted light. Soil never

needing overturning,
strawberries & raspberries emerge

layered in leaves and divine nectar.
Dragonflies skim ponds. Gulls

arc above the sea. There is no need
for paths, every surface a swath

to roam. The Earth
finally free. There was a before;

now there is an after.
The wind & the winged sing.

TRAVELING

and may you in your innocence/
sail through this to that ~ Lucille Clifton

Prepare for landing & finally breathe, so frightened I am
in the sky, that long, long arrow of fear above the clouds.
The mercy of new words for life and death – *from this to that.*

This, the dizzy, spinning Earth.

Luang Prabang is no longer a dot on a map
when I arrive in the heat on the muddy
banks of the Mekong. I kneel & bow,
my hands lift with rice and fruit for the monks.
I see the hems of orange folds
& hear the papery skin of their feet
on the narrow street.

I sit in a jeep so close to seven lions
eating the belly of a giraffe,
their open mouths bloodied caves,
the South African guide in front,
his gun glinting on the dashboard.

The quilt of rice paddies I bicycle along
& the Vietnamese bus driver who picks
a white flower on the roadside
to slip behind my ear.

In Rwanda, the smell of red dirt, dried fish,
battered metal, & the strange architecture
of forgiveness.

All this.

This afternoon I trapped a buzzing fly
between the window and screen.
I woke that night, moved down the dark stairs.
Lifted the window. Know that what is done
can sometimes be undone.

ON THE BANK

for Lucille Clifton

It took an hour
to memorize the lines,
ending with *sail*

through this to that –
learning a prayer,
following a tide

that pulls a boat into a river
that widens to an estuary,
and out to the Chesapeake Bay.

The horizon
of words inhaled,
granular, travel with blood and stay.

I look out at the white tipped sea,
taste the limestone air –
many lives in any one life

opening silently
in the wind –

AT NYAMATA

Insects hum.
Nothing forgotten.

Crows squawk,
children's candied voices

swell from a nearby school,
banana leaves sway and flap.

Inside emptied sleeves
and crumpled pants pile on pews.

Babies' blood rusts the walls
they were thrown against.

Down the road a new steeple
rises, unstained.

THAT'S WHAT IT IS

As if there was some treasure
map handed to us as we left
the womb. Find *this* – a big X
at the intersection
of want and need.

Is that what pandemic means –
to be squeezed into silence.

Remember that nine months
we had to conjure ourselves?
And now a return –
a swimming in quiet.

My name is breath.

Even in my tears
there is inhale
and exhale.
We are always
rising and falling.

HOPE RISING

The universal heft of stone
chips away with a mallet & chisel
& careful hands & tapping heart
just as we might do to a fossil
of knotted joy, the buried part
of hope. Let us feel the smooth
cave wall carve out what we know.
Know that we believe, still feel
what is hardened & rusted still.
This is not about discarding
but about finding the light dust
of cut granite, touching
the lines we make.

STONEWORK

I will come back to this world in a white cotton dress.
Kingdom after My Own Heart. Kingdom of Fragile. Kingdom of Dwarves.
— Lucie Brock-Broido

Everyone walks through shadows. Even the Queen of Mirrors
inside Mirrors in her Queendom of Sisters and Daughters.
Queendom of Umbilical Cords. Queendom of More.
I find more stones, more bones, more dust and ash
to unpack carefully like the heirloom baptismal dress
wrapped in tissue paper or the last leaf falling, leaving
branch roots against the sky, the ground turned upside down.
I keep unfolding, unmolding what aches to be retold.
The stone stacks I build and unbuild. The Queendom
of Cairns. Queendom of Water Marks.

So much compressed into a stone, the many stones
I've stolen, pieces of a place to remember being there.
I'd like to slice them like cake see the carbon of stars,
taste their light, the pumiced remains of eruptions,
the leathery skin of dinosaurs, the moonlight pressed into sea,
that first bite of an apple, that flesh and the stenciled fear
on cave walls, the making and unmaking of ruins
when the world was snow-filled then ice-covered, not even
one window of sadness left. Queendom of Unblemished.

I might find what I wanted all those hidden tears ago –
maybe the unfracture, a return to the ease of beginnings
before the shatter in the Queendom of Adjusting Well.
Queendom of Undressing. When my skin felt like a suit
with nothing underneath but a weightless kitten or the angel weight
of sorrow or nothing, nothing at all in the Queendom of No Corners.
Queendom of Pins Pursed in the Lips. Queendom of Sheets Drying

in Wind peopled by women who rinse rice, hold keys in their fists
in the dark, know about old failures and twisting rivers,
about opening gates and making gardens by lifting rocks.

Look, right there – one crow a silhouette
in the center of the road plucking at fresh death
as the last dash of sun gives even pebbles spikes of shadows
in the Queendom of Gravity and Orbit. I harness the work
of stones, fossick for evidence and remembrance,
unearth new moons. Queendom of Repair.

INDUSTRY

Maybe I am practicing for some god's commandments
with the chisel and mallet I tap across the smooth surface
of slate to unveil letters, carve words I can touch.
Or maybe I want to be a monk, transcribe the next bible,
as I memorize each compartment in the drawers of fonts,
align letters upside down onto a composing stick
before they are inked and pressed into paper.
Maybe we all just want to make something
close to sacred while we're here.
Once I watched a chipmunk drag some recyclables
one at a time into the emptiness of our ravine.
With closer inspection I saw the sun-flecked plastic bottles
peeking from a pile he'd camouflaged with leaves. So many
trips from our garage to create a glittering.

LETTERPRESSING IN AUTUMN, 2020

after Ada Limón

I set each sort upside down in the composing stick,
"A Name" emerging like the steady march of ice across our pond,
a dark openness lightening. In the wooden drawer
below I find the italicized letters for Eve's
whispered words: *Name me. Name me.*

Today I welcomed the unnamed, a billowing
or a deep murmuration as if the steeled depth of me
had been replaced or loosened back into itself.

It was like a single frond of a fern catching wind,
that kind of breathing freely, like what had tightened
released, first tears, then ease.

It was the fullness of a red maple,
the one on Jericho Street that makes an apron
of redness on the grass below when the sun
weaves through its generous branches,
a world unwobbling and settling,

and now from my window
I see a group of people on the crest of the ridge coming toward me.
I hear clinking glasses in their voices and in the late afternoon light,
that perfect slant of our star that rescues almost everything.
I see their faces now.

WE WERE HERE |

Did the dinosaurs bury their bones
for us to find, to dig up something
to name? My son knew every one,
had hard rubber versions he'd bring
in the car, invent worlds of before
in the backseat. How sturdy they were.
And his little legs, those, too.

Name the names.
Hold the bones. I promise
we were here.

UN/LOVE

AN INDEX OF SORROW

First, borrow the other word – pain,
the deep stitch that enters

in the knowing you will die.
Dogs and cats and squirrels

dig and eat and sleep unburdened.
Next, get closer to the surface

with the sting of unloved –
the one you wanted

who sentenced you
to heavy wings.

A shame – that hovers
and wraps its molecules,

no matter the thrashing
and rearranging you do

to displace what you know
to be true – a cloud

almost seen through.

GINGER ROOTS

I never saw them
in my mother's crowded kitchen,
but they remind me of her fingers
at the end, swollen knuckles, rings trapped –
the thin-skinned roots
I slice and sliver, simmer into sauces.
How what is unseen under the earth
can create a flavor I remember settling my stomach –
sipping the ginger ale she'd brought upstairs
and nibbling through a sleeve of Saltines
on the daybed in the TV room
while I watched "General Hospital"
inured to the squirrels scurrying in walls,
the first room I remember
finding how good my body felt
muffled and alone, so good
I thought I might get a disease
from the sharp rapture and release,
probably where I began
to see boys as a new landscape,
a place to lean against to unleash
what I didn't know but wanted.
Most good things grow in darkness –
seeds, roots, a fetus.

WITHOUT REGRET

The thrush chirps and flits
around my space when I invade
the place she's built her nest
for four tiny blue eggs, more candy than life.
I had to stop watering the hanging
flowering plant, watch it wither while
something hidden happened inside those eggs.
I chose the nest, didn't have to meditate on it
very long. I remember finding out
I was pregnant when I was too young.
I chose my life over what was beginning
to grow. I look up into the emptiness
and hush of the pewter sky, retrace
where I've been over and over again.

WHAT THE ASTRONAUT FINDS

The orbiting images before alphabets:
a stuffed monkey on a wire,
a tick burrowed into my neck,
a sister who felt like a twin
& the mumbled language we lived in
& lying in the back of the station wagon
looking out the wide window
to sky marbled by treetops,
always feeling like I was
flying downhill.

A sudden flicker of tender
pressure against the pen
as if the whorl of fingertips
remembers his skin & the heat
in the attic bedroom,
our young bodies naked
or nearly naked,
everywhere airless.

THE STRONG THREAD

Perhaps you know about the strong thread, the one that William Stafford
writes about that holds all your old dreams & your beforelife & your
afterlife the one that feels like breath or the beating cloud of a heart
that if you let it go you might die or fall into a life you don't want
like the one where you were drawn by nicotine to rummage through
ashtrays when no one was looking in search of a partially smoked
cigarette but of course someone was looking. You. You knew.
When you hold onto the strong thread, you unbury yourself.

BEFORE THE CURRENTS IN MY BLOOD BEGAN

To make another and let her grow,
before the pond was dug and filled by springs
before my parents' ashes lined its basin
before I loved the smoothness of red wine
before Shirley embroidered the wedding cloth
before we'd mapped the world with footprints and jet trails
before the large scars on my knees
before looking out this window framing trees and green,
I swam in a congregation of rivers
moved through sadness with a stomping
unbuttoned and buttoned soft shirts
and I knew when to say,
No. I am not ready.
No, I have a different life to live
how I sheltered myself inside myself
and walked down the hard cement steps
of a Planned Parenthood building
bleeding, yes, but knowing that the blood
would stop and life would open.
Call it 1980.
Call it my call.

MAYBE IT STARTED WITH THE COMPOSITION BOOK

In kindergarten, those thick spaces
and straight lines I filled and stayed on,
all the words I first learned to spell,
rhyming its own spell, releasing
a geyser: *call, tall, small*...
my hand another person,
someone strange and strong,
different from the little girl inside my skin,
then to the calligraphy set
under the Christmas tree,
that pen infusing a new language in me
as I held the nib at a slant
to create a new dimension.
Onto carving in slate
and the letterpress
and drawers of fonts.
What stays on a page
or a stone is like saving a moth,
the flutter inside my palms
until I release it to live in the night.
I touch carved letters, press the scar
to feel the healing.
My mother always works her way
onto the page tying or untying an apron
No, I have not lettered her gravestone
though she lines the basin
of our pond. I dive into the past,
swim in her ashes and bits of bone
and plant words in furrowed rows,
surprised by what grows.

THE PARADE

Imagine that we could pick our mothers that there was a parade
of them walking by and we stand behind some gentle barrier
to watch and select from the mothers who carry spools of thread
and pins pursed in their lips the ones whose fingers smell of onions
and garlic the resolute who iron their sheets the scent of steamed
cotton following them like perfume the strong and rural with chickens
and goats close behind the ones with buckets of plastic dinosaurs
and dolls weighted in their arms the dreamers with moons for eyes
and stories about space and weightlessness the ones who know
about waves and the shore and we could choose the one who
looks at us with eyes like mirrors that say *I want you*
as she bends down reaches out a hand and we realize
that we are not choosing that we are the one being picked
and loved just because we came to the parade what if
we knew how much we were wanted the way
I did years later when I finally found you.

TEMPLE

I believed I needed the robed monks
to unearth the secret of inner peace
maybe under a stone I couldn't lift
or swivel free. I followed their dust
in the hills of Chiang Mai province,
in the open temples on the banks
of the Ganges, and kneeling
with cupped palms full of rice
and mango as alms at dawn in Laos.

But this morning standing in my shower
in Vermont seeing how much of me is skin
and under the warm water, I breathed in
a world – those who laid the pipes,
smoothed the grout over fresh placed tile,
the hands that weaved the towel I wrapped
around myself, and on the wall of the fogged room
the print a student made and framed.

INHABITING AN ANT

after Ross Gay

The hunger of it,
the grip, even when
it is upside down.
The smallness,
the finding of an opening
in a box of sugar, that endless sweetness
and in this way I feel fine
when it slips unhit into darkness
between the counter and stove,
and in this way we survive
side by side my hand silenced
as I watch another find its way
up the steep wall
of the smooth ceramic sink,
climb with an ease
I wanted in Patagonia,
my backpack snug
against my body,
my poles a part of my arms
scaling rocky inclines,
moving in unimaginable beauty
so far from this kitchen,
in unbroken land
skirting turquoise lakes
under clouds collecting
like a partition above.
Wind everywhere.

INTERPRETER

More mountain than sea,

       sky.   Signs, these birds.

Through a metal slot on Central Avenue,
      a *Highlights* magazine

      Find what's hidden in the tree trunks:

I have to die.   Along the dirt road, *Look up!*

Three crows.   Sugar Top Road,
            a cloud of swallows.

    Last night in the bathroom my husband heard flapping
thought it was rain on the skylight, felt something brush
by his head, whipped it away.

        Small pile of thin wings
on the floor before it lifted. He closed the door.

      Waited.

Bat on soap dish. Until wrapped in towel, flung outside.

In our bed its heart in his eyes.

GOD

That vibration in the space
between me and someone I love,
or don't love or don't even know,
like a stranger sitting next to me
on a plane and we find we have the same
book and I tell her a secret I've never told anyone
and when I take my bag from overhead
and walk on earth again, she stays,
as if my blood and bones feel her,
and it's the pulsing between
me and my children,
one in the beginning,
a shared skin
the divine etched in,
but even when they grow and leave
and return, the shine of their hair
in my palm and when we embrace,
I breathe them in,
and with you, my love,
that shuddering, shimmering –
how impossible and luminous
over decades, an invisible fire.

MY ANATOMY

Did I have two hearts –
one for loving bad boys
and one for loving the kind ones?

Too many summer secrets
with the bad ones when we jumped
into random pools and I took off
most of my clothes on a golf course
at night, always at night with them
that aching heart
that couldn't get enough
of a two-sudden love.

These were not breakfast boys,
no light-of-day, no, they stayed
in the chambers of dark dream and distance,
exhausting that heart.

Thank god for you
and that clean heart
starting its thrum.

Thank god the sun rises –
how bright and warm
and forgiving everything becomes.

RIDDLES

Take nine, multiply it by three,
subtract seven, divide by four,
what's the number now?
my mind moving
like lightning for you
as we sat at the dining room table,
the creaking wood, that could squeeze
more leaves into its stretching.

Each morning I walk outside,
inhale the scent of wild mint
that fringes the forest,
the call of a rooster, the bark
of one dog. I need the dirt beneath
my feet, the leaves just out of reach,
the wind as harvest – what sweeps
below the skin and takes me in.
Where are you now? I ask no one.

A YOUNG MAN SITS BESIDE ME ON THE STONE BENCH AT THE KILLING FIELDS

He must have a mother, somewhere
incredulous that the baby she held,

(once with intention and fierceness
as she slipped down fourteen steps

with him in her arms) that fragile
cargo, has a beard

& travels the world
without her.

DAYBREAK

Muscling in the blinds
in lines of light,

the sun sharpens
your shoulder blades

as you sleep. I wake
with banners of words pulled

through a sea-side sky,
lift the covers' wide wing.

There is no quiet like morning,
no center flowering

like a journal opening.
I feel another symmetry

when I surrender
to the small gods.

GIVING THANKS

This morning I awoke in gratitude
actually said aloud, *Thank you, Ambien, Mom, Dad,*
and God (just in case), my husband already stretching
and exercising after checking for limp-tailed prostrate
mounds of fur in the traps he'd set the night before
and takes them to a place I only imagine.
The sad scatter of tiny skeletons.
I will let a mouse scurry on the floors
and in drawers long before I'll pick up
that small quietness and wing it into woods.

Not all death I avoid – as a hospice volunteer,
I have felt the last beat of more than one heart,
touched stilled skin that lacquers as it leaves,
believe that death and birth share a world.

I should thank him first. Before the relief of sleep,
before my dead parents, before a deity I do not know.
He is the person who saved a different me
more swelled with need, not exactly like the helicopter
that lifted the lobsterman from Montauk after hours
of treading dark water with only a small buoy
but like that.

MAKING SENSE

1.
How long I've wanted
to capture something,
render the unsyllabled,
put a lid on what I love
as if the small, dark lines
and curves on a page will burst
into the flesh of a ripe peach,
as if my teeth could speak
about the puncture of soft,
furred skin and I am here
with my eyelids wide open
in this marred world,
how it feels
like a paradise
and then a morass.

I stopped eating meat
because of the blood
and then because I read
about veal: a calf killed,
its whole short life tied
to a certain spot so that no
tough muscle forms
from movement.

2.
And the little flickers
in the glass jar –
were they sending messages,
to other creatures,

forewarning of little humans
skipping on night grass,
bare feet silent and cool?

IN SEARCH OF

1.
As if we were all small owls
clutching a branch
in a world turned sideways,
our tree severed and moving
on a truck heading to some city
in December.

2.
I hold the trolls I loved
their long colorful hair,
the larger half of a wishbone
with the wish, and the Archie comic book
I read over and over, a life
I wanted in its thin pages.

3.
How easily the leaves give into wind
but not to falling; some stubborn ones
rattle all winter so tight the bond.
None of us should drown.

4.
Move under the shadows of the unpeeled leaves
of the artichoke to find the generous heart.

5.
Crouched in the barn under a roof
sagging into a rusted car, the upright
but broken wooden wheelchair,
a filing cabinet with one drawer
pulled out as if someone might return –

6.
Remember the smooth pennies you pulled from the train tracks,
thin and warm with near-death.

7.
And Rilke who told a young poet to dive
into aloneness.

8.
Think of the waterfall
not just the roar but the pool below, the one that
encased the fawn who either slipped or leapt from the edge.

9.
Find what you coil inside.

THANK YOU

My gratitude extends to a village of poets who have generously read my work and made it better: Wendy Drexler, Margot Wizansky, Vivian Eyre, Cynthia Bargar, Steve Nickman, Xiaoly Li, Connemara Wadsworth, Anastasia Vassos, Laura Foley, Peggy Brightman, Jill Herrick-Lee, Deb Franzoni, John Escher, Pam Ahlen, Wendy Smith, Lynne Byler, Joanne Durham, Jayne Marek, Eileen Cleary, Kelly Dumar, Christine Jones, Miriam O'Neal, Annie Pluto, Gloria Monaghan, Hermine Meinhard, Frances Donovan, Anna V. Q. Voss, Jennifer Martelli, Erica Charis-Molling, Melissa McKinstry, Judith Fox, Annie Hampford, Elizabeth Tan, and Carol Young. To my mentors: Barbara Helfgott Hyatt, Ellen Bass, Frank X. Gaspar, Marie Howe, Traci Brimhall, Kelli Russell Agodon, and Kim Addonizio. My sisters, too. And of course, to my children, Abby and David (and the lovely people they are marrying, Paul and Emily).

And mostly to you, Ben, my everything.

ABOUT THE AUTHOR

Sarah Dickenson Snyder lives in Vermont, carves in stone, & rides her bike. Travel opens her eyes. She has four poetry collections, *The Human Contract (2017), Notes from a Nomad* (nominated for the Massachusetts Book Awards *2018*), *With a Polaroid Camera (2019)* and *Now These Three Remain* (2023). Poems have been nominated for Best of Net and Pushcart Prizes. Her work is in *Rattle, Lily Poetry Review*, and *RHINO*. sarahdickensonsnyder.com

CPSIA information can be obtained
at www.ICGtesting.com
Printed in the USA
JSHW080917210523
41985JS00003B/154